Submissive's Guide To BDSM Vol. 1

66 Tips On How To Enjoy Happy & Healthy BDSM Relationship As A Sub

Matthew Larocco

Submissive's Guide To BDSM Vol. 1

Publisher: Enlightened Publishing

ISBN-13: 978-1533120922

ISBN-10: 1533120927

Disclaimer

The Publisher has strived to be as accurate and complete as possible in the creation of this book. While all attempts have been made to verify information provided in this publication, the Publisher assumes no responsibility for errors, omissions, or contrary interpretation of the subject matter herein. Any perceived slights of specific persons, peoples, or organizations are unintentional.

This book is not intended for use as a source of legal, business, accounting or financial advice. All readers are advised to seek services of competent professionals in the legal, business, accounting, and finance fields.

The information in this book is not intended or implied to be a substitute for professional medical advice, diagnosis or treatment. All content contained in this book is for general information purposes only. Always consult your healthcare provider before carrying on any health program.

Table of Contents

Introduction

"You've done something wrong. Something very bad. And because of that, you are going to have to be punished severely."

Depending on the context of that statement, that's either really good news or really bad news. If that's a teacher in a grammar school talking to your kid, it's bad news. If it's a cop or a lawyer it's definitely a bad thing.

But if you're a consenting adult and your punisher is a sexy "Dom" then chances are, you're really going to enjoy this relationship based on punishment.

Much of what we see in BDSM practice, especially in the mainstream, focuses on how to become dominant and act like the ideal Dom or Master, or "Top." However, a lot of newcomers are confused as to how this works. They vaguely understand that the submissive or sub or slave is supposed to obey. But they don't understand the emotional dynamics, or how to act like the ideal sub, or even how to enjoy the experience.

After all, spanking or any kind of corporal punishment is not pleasurable just on its own. Ask any kid that and he / she will agree, spankings are painful and terrifying at that age. However, with the emotional adult dynamic, and the complexity of human psychology, these spankings and other forms of punishment can be a very erotic experience for you.

In fact, before you become a Dom, it's usually recommended that you experience BDSM as a sub so that you can personally "feel" what your sub is going to feel. That way, you will not abuse your sub and chase all your playmates away. Furthermore, you will understand the emotional nuances that are necessary to make punishment truly pleasurable and not just injurious.

So think of the power dynamic of Top and Bottom like a Taser or a Stun Gun. In order to realize the great power that you have as a Dom, it's best that you experience firsthand just how a "little" can be a "lot".

That's what this book is going to teach you. How to be a better sub, not a Dom.

And not only why you "have to do it" but more importantly, why being a sub is the far better deal in the BDSM lifestyle. So let's start talking about what a bad boy / bad girl you've been lately. Shall we?

Note: For the sake of simplicity, all Doms are referred to as He and all subs are referred to as She. However, sexes are interchangeable.

Chapter 1: Why You Want to Experience Punishment

Being the sub or more specifically…

- The Bottom or "Baby" (A newcomer to the lifestyle)

- The Sub or Student (An intermediate player)

- The Slave (A very experienced naughty fellow)

…means quite simply that you want to be the star of the show. The Dom is going out of his way and working hard to make you feel exactly what you desire to feel. So while the Dom has to fulfill the role of…

- The Top or "Daddy"

- The Dom (Domme) or Teacher

- The All Powerful "Master

Everything he does is to help and entertain you. The Dom has the more difficult role, since he has to create scenes and design a sort of "curriculum" of punishment that will arouse you and satiate you. You have the task of simply sitting back, doing as you're told, and enjoying the fun.

Of course, once you sense that a Dom doesn't know what he's doing, it's time for you to speak up and end the relationship. This is a common problem, especially among women wishing to be dominated by men. Men usually take this dominant attitude as an excuse to just cause pain upon women, and usually women they don't understand or perhaps even hate.

They don't understand the "love" factor of BDSM. They don't understand the necessity of learning each individual person and catering the punishment to please THEM, the sub, and not simply to arouse the Dom. They fail to understand what is at the heart of BDSM as a culture and lifestyle, and that is not necessarily "pain" but the *equal* balance of power.

Power is What Motivates Pain and Pleasure

Tip #1: In this kind of relationship, one partner must always exercise power over the other.

We spend so much time indoctrinating children, teaching them the importance of equality between men and women and all ethnicities and cultures. And while this is the right thing to do, being "right" and kind doesn't always make for an exciting sex life. To some extent, we all want what we can't have...and in this case, that means sexual or non-sexual BDSM experiences that allow us to feel a type of love that is grossly unbalanced and dysfunctional.

In a normal relationships, these power imbalanced relationships are considered abusive or insane—we help people to leave these destructive relationships. However, in BDSM these relationships are forged with consent in mind, as well as a number of stipulations that protect both partners.

Therefore, as a sub your intent is to find someone that will hold power over you. It's not enough to maintain power (as in a household where the man wears the "pants" in the family) but to actually USE that power in a demonstrable way. Specific actions that the Dom takes, wielding his power, will allow him to direct and guide your scale of pain and pleasure.

You only consent to allow the relationship to start and continue and to set out any ground rules about what you cannot endure. As we discussed in the *Dom's Guide to BDSM* series, the Dom does not have unlimited power over the sub. The sub tells the Dom about limitations and goals in advance. That way, the Dom can avoid injuring the sub by pushing them beyond what they can bear.

We also discussed the influence of Freud and even Marquis de Sade on the science of BDSM, or as it was once understood: sadism and masochism. Interestingly, when the old world "pioneers" of this behavior were at work, consent was not really a focus. There were no rules among partners, only the vague understanding that inflicting physical and emotional pain can cause joy to the dominant partner and that some victims of the pain would have an orgasmic reaction.

Leopold von Sacher-Masoch wrote of the understanding as the "sub" or the antiquated version of the sub. Freud came up with the concept of explaining pleasure and pain from the childhood dynamic, though he considered kinks "diseases" from an incorrect development of child psyche. For much of BDSM's history, and still today, many doctors view it as a form of pathology, or at least a disorder.

However, to think of it only as Sadism and Masochism would be oblivious to the new age concepts of Bondage, Submission, Sadism and Masochism, or sometimes called Dominance and Submission. It's like a dance—one partner is dominant, but that only works if the partner is a *willing* sub.

Tip #2: The sub must always be trusting of the Dom, and in the cases of meeting new Tops, she must give him the chance to prove himself.

Much like other disciplines, from psychology to hypnosis, the efficacy of BDSM requires a willing partner. You as a sub cannot "resist" your Dom to the extent that he becomes frustrated and gives up. Most Doms are simply not strong enough or patient enough to deal with a "difficult sub." They may even find it insulting to the lifestyle, if you consider yourself a sub but cannot take orders or sincerely play the scene as needed.

The Dom is not required to be an unbreakable machine of machismo. He has feelings too and if he feels he is being taken advantage of, or that his sub is constantly arguing with him, he will walk away. Then guess what? You're a sub no one wants to work with.

Naturally, because of the potential for severe abuse, the modern community has instituted the policy of contracts and oral agreements in advance of the "scene," to ensure that this partnership is still "equal" within the rights of human beings, even while playing with uneven power roles. You are, after all, just acting—method acting for your own learning experience and pleasure. Nobody is actually holding a person hostage or gaining power over their mind.

This is precisely why Doms and subs are advised to create a written and agreed upon contract, so that there is no misunderstanding.

In fact, don't risk it. Write everything out in a contract and agree upon it, sign it and save it somewhere. That way, oral agreements are not needed. Trust is assured and if there is any chicanery or poor performance by a Dom, you can fire him for violating the contract as agreed upon.

Tip #3: Let your Dom feel like a Man.

Or in the case of a gender reversal, let her feel like a woman. In other words, a master, a Top and a Teacher with unlimited power.

While you both know that there are limits, you must believe for the sake of the scene that your Dom really does have full control over you and there's no "going back." You are his to control, to punish and to train according to whatever method he feels is necessary.

The contract explains in detail what will and will not occur, but usually subs are very impressed when the Dom presents himself as unpredictable, powerful and all too convincing when it comes to showing his menacing side. The Dom is a good actor and you should be an even better actor, capable of making him feel totally confident and in control of you.

If you don't put yourself out there and "try" – to feel terrified, to feel aroused, to feel punished and helpless – then the dynamic will not be right and the scene will suffer. Besides, inexperienced Doms are simply not as skilled as old pros. Just a little bit of awkward tension or poor performance coming from you, will knock them off their game and they will lose their confidence. Some might even become angry and resort to being violent or intimidat-

ing, and that's going to be the end of the relationship.

A Superiority Complex

Simply put, all Doms must have a superi-
ority complex of some sort for the scene to
work. Some will simply think they are Sex
Gods, while others believe they are dungeon
masters and that they "own" their slaves.
Some may think of themselves as stern teach-
ers ready to discipline their student or as the
"boss" who has financial control of the em-
ployee.

Of course, for newcomers to the scene, a
much easier level to start with is the role of a
parent. The Dom will consider himself a loving father here to discipline you and ultimately make you feel good by submitting to his authority.

This puts special emphasis on you as the
sub to...

Tip #4: Obey him and show respect.

Subs must submit to the authority of the
Dom and must be submissive to his personality in every way. In the old 1940s era of domi-

nant husbands over wives, this meant treating the wife as a child or as a servant of the house. While much of the population has abandoned that model, the same lessons apply in a pseudo romantic relationship of roles.

The Dom deserves complete obedience, and without any "challenges" coming from the sub. You as the sub don't argue with the Dom while in the scene – unless you want to specifically request to be punished for speaking up. In most cases, the sub simply obeys without question and does not raise her voice, as would a rebellious wife.

The sub shows respect, meaning she does not undermine the Dom or show a lackadaisical response. If she laughs or if she doesn't take the instructions seriously, she will be punished or perhaps even fired by the Dom. Showing respect is about attitude. Have a healthy fear of displeasing the Dom is the sub's primary motivation. She fears his punishment just as she fears losing his love and his rewards.

Tip #5: Don't do act or think unless directed.

You are never allowed to speak unless spoken to and asked a question. This is because attitude means everything and you taking action, without asking permission, is showing disrespect to the Dom who now controls your every move.

The Dom will oftentimes demand to be called Sir, Ma'am, Master, Mistress or another title. This is so that you will take a respectful attitude when addressing him or her and not feel entitled to communicate with him or her as an equal. Because in the BDSM scenario you are not equal. Whether you know that right away or have to be educated as to your inferiority over time, will be up to you and the Dom to decide.

While it's not very easy to refrain from "thinking" as a sub, you WILL find that if you simply stop over-thinking the situation and learn to simply *experience*, you will get a lot more out of the training.

BDSM operates on a level that is emotional and almost visceral. Over thinking it and trying too hard will work against you. So rather than justify it, rather than question your Dom, just submit. He will do the thinking for you and the experience will be very good in the hands of the right Dom.

In the next chapter, we're going to bring on the pain. What does pain mean in this context and how do you "enjoy" pain when it's actually causing you stress? Let's proceed into Chapter 2.

Chapter 2: The Science of Pain

What is pain? We all know how it feels. And true, we usually fear pain and go out of our way to avoid it. One of the most common misconceptions about BDSM is that subs just want to be abused and suffer through pain. This is not really the case, with the possible exception of extreme masochism.

In reality, what the sub wants is to feel the intensity of an uncomfortable experience and then feel the *endorphin and adrenaline rush* that comes from ceasing that pain. Pain is often defined as intense or damaging stimuli. However, it's important to remember that pain is often subjective.

That means that not everyone experiences pain in the same way. What might be unbearable to you, may be pleasurable or tolerable to someone else. Some may even find minor instances of pain to be titillating. Therefore, in the community, "pain" as is the classic definition, is usually second to power, humiliation and a sort of push and pull approach to pleasure.

The Dom gives you pleasure and pain and without both, you cannot truly appreciate pleasure. For many subs, dominance and pleasure may be enough. For others, they may crave more emotional or physical stimuli, perhaps even temporarily painful experiences. The old expression goes, if you haven't experienced pain and if you haven't had pleasure taken away from you, you cannot truly appreciate receiving pleasure.

So depending on your preferences and endurance, you may want to rely on the push and pull system of discipline—receiving some pleasure and then receiving stimuli that takes away that pleasure—or actual punishment, which focuses on pain.

If it's the latter, and you and your Dom agree to bring pain into the scene, you will be operating according to Subspace theory.

Subspace—The Name of the Pain Game

Enduring pain would be pointless and miserable if not for the *chemical reaction* happening in your body during and after experiencing the pain. Even the anticipation of pain coming is a vital part to creating deep emotion. And no doubt, emotion and physical reaction will both be involved in creating a pleasurable session that's beyond just "kink" and more into the amazing out of body experience that everyone craves.

When you experience pain, just as with exercise, you feel an endorphins rush that is similar to a runner's high or perhaps the afterglow of orgasm.

If the "threshold" is just barely reached or only slightly surpassed, then the sub will experience adrenaline, which creates a state of mind known as subspace. This state, comparable to a trance, renders the sub lethargic, orgasmic and almost childlike in response.

An experienced Dom will know how to take you to subspace and it will involve a certain number of time period of painful stimuli, followed a period of release and a ceasing of punishment. During the release, the adrenaline hits you. When that wears off, punishment commences until the next rest and release section.

While you are in control of whatever happens, always remember:

Tip #6: Give the Dom some creative leeway, in determining what punishments are appropriate. Don't disqualify anything unless you know it's too extreme for you.

You have the task of disqualifying certain acts and behaviors early on when drawing up the contract. However, once you do submit to your Dom, you are usually not the one who comes up with a curriculum. The Dom's job is to create sessions that will continually push you closer to an emotional and physical subspace peak.

If you are not sure about something, don't disqualify it too early. Simply explain that you have limited experience in it and would like to take it slow. This way, your Dom will know to start with something simple and to *try a wider variety of techniques* until you both find something you like.

Many subs are not aware of what will work, and if they have no real BDSM experience, they are counting on the Dom to come up with creative ideas.

Tip #7: Rather than dismissing something you feel uneasy about, try organizing the list into degrees.

You can assign numbers, from 0 (never want to try it) to 5 (love it!) or something similar to that method of rating. Breaking down your likes and dislikes into more helpful guidelines for which to create scenarios will help the Dom to learn you and how he can approach the threshold of pain. An example might look like this.

- Pinching 5
- Scratching 3
- Using Teeth 3
- Spanking 5
- Whipping 4
- Burning (as with wax) 2
- Ice Cubes 2
- Sharp Wheels 2
- Bondage Gear 5
- Sex Toys 4
- Electronic Stimulation 2

You can also add in other staples of eroticism such as dirty talking, role playing, lifestyles and so on.

Tip #8: Study the Dom's behavior and/or contract which details curriculum.

This is important because at some point you have to critically analyze the Dom to get a sense of where he is going with these sessions. If he is not well organized or doesn't quite understand the dynamic of power exchange then it's a waste of time. There's no reason to continue, nor to "trust him" if it's obvious he doesn't know what he's doing.

For example, the power exchange *requires* discipline. It requires training and specific instructions that must be followed, or else there will be punishment. If the sub follows through on these instructions she will be rewarded. This is essentially part of the push and pull system, the educational aspect of BDSM, which is often ignored among new Doms.

You as the sub will not fully learn or enjoy the sessions if there is no discipline and especially in situations involving pain.

The reality of this is observed in parental model, with obligations towards children. No sane or normal parent abuses their child just for pleasure. And this doesn't just mean corporal punishment but also in dispensing emotional discipline. The child will grow up with major disorders and perhaps even disassociation from the abuse or the neglect.

On the other hand, if one trains a child in love, then the training helps them to become a better person in adulthood.

Strange as it may seem, the same is true in the science of BDSM. The Dom disciplines with intent. To re-shape the sub's thinking into a more practical way of living.

Therefore, analyze the Dom's behavior, or if possible get a hold of his contract, his "program" or schedule, and perhaps even his references from other subs. This will give you the *confidence* that you need to *fully submit and give him your trust*.

When a Dom knows what he's doing and you fully trust him, respect him, and obey, that's the dynamic that makes pain possible and that can quite literally rock your world and give a once in a lifetime experience.

In addition to signing the contract, determine a safe word that you are comfortable with, or perhaps a series of safe words that could mean, stop, slow down and keep going.

Tip #9: Take care of yourself and don't expose yourself to "real life" pain.

This is very important, especially given how many Doms are so engrossed in their character that they neglect the little things—like making sure the sub is comfortable and in good health!

This means not only establishing rules in advance but also ensuring that common sense laws are in effect. This means getting an STD test in advance and making sure the Dom has done so, if sexual intercourse is expected. Immunization shots are also a good idea, to prevent exposure to Hepatitis A and B, HPV, and other prevalent infections.

Safe words are a given, but what about silent alarms that indicate you are at an emergency level, but cannot communicate the safe word? A good Dom will be able to sense this, but YOU have to take the initiative and warn him that if you cannot speak (usually because of a subspace high) you will give him a silent alarm signal; such as a shake of the head, a tap or touch, a wink, or whatever action you can do while under duress so he knows to slow it down or stop.

Another good idea is to take a CPR class and or make sure the Dom knows CPR in case you stop breathing or experience another medical scare. Obviously, there should be protocol in place if there is a medical emergency, or a fainting, or excessive bleeding, and the like. DO NOT assume the Dom will take care of this and be disappointed. Make sure that he has such a plan in place and if he doesn't be VERY wary about approaching a subspace peak with an unqualified Dom.

In other words, offer your full trust only to Doms who deserve it. You as a sub have the task of choosing which Doms you will submit to and the sooner you realize, that VERY FEW will actually qualify and meet your high standards, the better.

In the next chapter, we're going to discuss the importance of why you should work as a sub regardless of whether you want pleasure or you want further training.

Chapter 3: Why You Need to Experience Life as a Sub as Training for a Dom

It is true that many Doms are only talented at being in charge, whereas many subs simply cannot lead—they only want to be instructed and disciplined. While there are "switches" that can play both roles, it is essential to at least understand the point of view of the sub, even if you are the Dom.

Not only is this to protect the sub, since the Dom does owe the sub protection, love and empathy, but it also has to do with under-standing a person's desires. At some point, you realize that you have peripheral desires (attractions, types and kinks) but you also have *hidden* desires—taboo thoughts and sen-sations that you may not have even realized you had.

The only way to explore these hidden desires and reach thresholds you never even knew you could endure is to submit to someone who can bring you to that point.

So yes to some extent, you are not just looking for someone who respects your rules...

Tip #10: You want to find a Dom that has experience in pushing the boundaries of those rules without going overboard.

And usually that experience comes not from instinct but from actually having submitted himself to his own Domme in previous relationships. He knows exactly how much stress, discipline and punishment it takes to test boundaries but still respect prerequisites of the contract.

Too much recklessness will traumatize the sub, but an overly cautious handling may be too dull for the sub to fully enjoy the experience.

Tip #11: If you ever do go on to be a Dom, you can learn how to be protective of others from your own experiences.

There are so many unqualified Doms out there you're doing the community a favor by learning and teaching your Doms, as a smart sub, the importance of protection and fantasy fulfillment and not just mindless sex.

You can actually give your Dom clues, hints and alarm signals that will help him improve his response time, his behavior and his guidance. A newcomer sub simply experiences new things and learns from them. A really smart sub actually helps the Dom improve his craft and become better in serving other subs.

A Shared Mindset

Ideally, you want to share a mindset of trust and maximum arousal as this well help you, almost instinctively, to learn each other and do your best in each scene. Basically put, achieving the same mindset requires good communication (both explicit in the negotiation phase and the aftercare), verbal and non-verbal cues during the action, and trust.

However, new subs may be confused as to how they feel trust and display trust, thereby showing the Dom they are supportive.

Therefore, take these tips to heart as to how YOU as the sub should be prepared in mind, and how this attitude directly affects the Dom. If you play to "switch" or learn the sub's role before becoming a Dom, that's even better.

Tip #12: Be emotionally stable, as if in a real life relationship.

This is a bit of an underreported problem in newcomers to BDSM; many subs join the community because they are emotional wrecks and need someone to guide them back to health. This can be dangerous however, and not only because there are really awful Doms out there waiting to prey upon the weak and vulnerable.

But in theory, you need to fix yourself before you allow yourself to trust, to "love" as it were, even though your definition of love may vary from that of others. The truth is that many newcomers to BDSM should be taking time out from relationships with others until they (A) get over a breakup, (B) get over their desperation, and (C) get over their loneliness. Adding complication to your already shattered ego, only amplifies negative feelings.

And the unfortunate fact is that subs who are "confused" in life oftentimes don't know what they want from a Dom – and that definitely creates problems unless you happen to meet the one elusive "Dom with a Heart of Gold and a Streak of Genius." And yeah, he's about as commonly seen as Prince Charming.

Tip #13: Being a good sub means you are ready and CAPABLE of being honest.

Subs who are screwed up in the head from real life drama or trauma are not truly capable of being honest or emotionally naked. They may hide truths, exaggerate or distort the truth, or even deny wrongdoing on their own part. If you can't be honest with your Dom, you cannot trust. You're not ready for any of this.

Tip #14: A good sub accepts responsibility.

A good sub accepts responsibility for their mistakes and admits whenever she is wrong. Now this isn't just a matter of showing respect or deference to the Dom's will. This means being honest with yourself and being courageous enough to admit it, "out of character" and not just in character.

You may be wrong about one of your thresholds or limits. You may learn that you are not ready for something you thought you were, or may have doubted the Dom's opinion about something in training.

Just because you're running the show, don't be too proud to admit the Dom was right and you were wrong. Everybody makes mistakes and the sooner they own up to it, the sooner trust can be reestablished.

Tip #15: Subs don't just want pleasure or pain. They want to PLEASE their Dom.

This works in reverse too, as the Dom has an earnest desire to please the sub. You will both reach a comfortable shared mindset when both of you are seeking to please the other partner.

Really good Doms are not looking for "doormats" or pushovers they can abuse and mistreat. The really good Doms want someone that understands their own desires and needs, as well as what they can do to please someone else. Thinking of how you can please your Dom will earn his trust.

A good sub chooses to submit and is happy about it. They usually don't have to be "broken down" except in extreme scenarios.

This is also a good way to gauge whether your Dom is working out or not. Is he still forcing you to do something or are you actually enjoying following his orders? If not, then the dynamic is off and it's probably time to end the relationship or at least renegotiation some aspects of it.

And for that matter…

Tip #16: Have the guts to say NO.

Just because you're a sub doesn't mean you have to submit to every Dom who makes an offer or who "orders" you to take him on. If you become a doormat and go with whoever asks you, you will not be establishing trust. You will be putting yourself at great risk, since many Doms have very low standards and poor technique.

The bottom line is that you should create a series of qualifications so that most Doms WILL NOT qualify to be your Top. We'll discuss these standards in a later chapter. But start thinking about this now…the kind of Dom you want and the kind you don't need.

Tip #17: Be willing to communicate. Ask for what you need and what you want.

Remember that aftercare and pre-scene negotiation is all about open and explicit communication. There is also plenty of room for "in character" communication, but it's best to speak honestly after the scene so you can tell the Dom if you need extra time, or if you want to explain a feeling you have or a fantasy you want to explore.

There may be a "mystery" to solve, as regards what you actually want and what your threshold is. Maybe you need a long conversation to talk out what you think the issue is, or maybe you're feeling rebellious or unhappy about something and want to complain. This is all healthy, assuming it's not during the scene. Since all of this deals with highly emotional moments, and not always "logical" solutions, the two of you may have to discuss various ideas and brainstorm a bit.

The Dom isn't a mind reader and even the good ones don't know your secret thoughts if you don't share them or at least share "clues" as to what's going on inside your head, even if you don't know yourself. So don't sabotage the relationship by expecting too much from a

Dom that is hard trying to please you, but can only work at his unique capacity.

Tip #18: Keep a journal of your activities.

Lastly, keep a record of your activities and not just the contract. Record not only what you did but also the experiences and emotions that you had working with the Dom. This will help you get out all your thoughts and feelings. It may also help you to voice your concerns better if you can refer to the journal and get specifics on the scene when you need to re-negotiate.

Keeping records can also help the Dom immensely, as he can take down notes about what the sub has revealed about herself via direct conversation, or perhaps just in casual conversation. A really smart Dom will use all of this information, including little notes and observations, in helping to please the sub.

Chapter 4: The Most Taboo Experiences You'll Ever Find

Sex—all it really is on a scientific level is procreation, though human beings and a couple of other animals have evolved to actually enjoy the act for pleasure. Therefore, it comes as no surprise that sex becomes a bit boring whenever a couple gets used to a routine. In theory, the most erotic experiences of one's life come when you are able to pass a threshold of eroticism and surpass the boundaries of what you're comfortable, eventually reaching a peak of sexual excitement.

Eroticism, classically defined, involves not only sexual desire but also romance and sensuality. The French novelist Honore de Balzac once wrote that one's erotic identity is formed not only by his or her own code of morality, but also the culture and the environment in which that person lives. This also includes the time period, as a number of ages were associated with either sexual repression or sexual revolution.

And to some extent, eroticism is about making the private and taboo thoughts inside your own mind public. Another French philosopher (surprise, the French know about eroticism!) was named Georges Bataille, and he stated that not only was eroticism about a person being "in conflict with himself," but that it was also a "psychological quest," not just physical activity.

Indeed, that is the heart of it. You can use all the sex toys you want and try any position you want, but ultimately what turns you on and brings you to new heights of passion is the erotic thought process.

A man or woman in conflict with themselves means, simply put, that you want what you can't have. Your entire identity comes from numerous thoughts and attitudes that make you unique and give you your own sense of morals and values. Therefore, to betray the values that you have, would be to feel guilt—as if you have sinned or have "sold out" to the morals you thought you had.

You may never sell out or betray your own conscience in real life but in a sexual fantasy, you would normally be far less inhibited, and thus would explore another world involving you, and a world where you act very uncharacteristically to your own nature.

At the same time, you are bored with what you can get. So while you may find the idea of meeting a true love, or finding someone you are morally and intellectually compatible with, in the back of your minds dark thoughts may float around, involving sex with the wrong type of person or the relationships you really don't want because they involve too much risk, pain or emotional injury.

Even though your conscience rejects these sexual experiences, your subconscious still finds them appealing because it represents the temptation of a new life, a new adventure.

So one of the first rules of finding new taboos to exploit would be…

Tip #19: Figure out who you are and what values are most precious to you.

You cannot truly challenge yourself sexually until you know yourself internally. A lack of introspection and a misunderstanding of who you are and what you represent are the most common reasons why people have boring sex lives.

Now it is usually your Dom's job to help figure out what kind of scenarios challenge you, but the truth is, your sexual adventures will be much more fun if you know this in advance.

If you can tell the Dom straight out what you enjoy, you will make his job easier...and he will be able to put more thought into scenarios and less thought having to learn your complicated mind. If you only have newbie Doms or B-level Doms to work with, then even more pressure is put upon you to make this relationship work.

So try this exercise: write down the most important characteristics that make you unique and remind you of who you are inside.

An example might look like this:

- I have a family but they are second to my selfish desires

- I believe in taking pleasure or punishment from other people, not caring about them

- I believe in being respectful only to those who meet my requirements

- I believe in helping only to those who meet my requirements

- I like people who are aggressive; I like lying and cheating because it's convenient

- I don't deserve to be treated the same way as everyone else

These are just some examples of how you would create "opposite desires" based on your opposite traits. Whereas the real life you is a kind person, the "evil you" is selfish and enjoys destructive relationships that make no logical sense.

These are what most would consider normal morals or values. However, they make for a comfortable life—not a sexually adventurous one.

Now that you know what you are, and recognize your most basic traits, let's try corrupting them.

Tip #20: Destroy your morals...invent a "new lifestyle" that allows you to behave in ways contrary to your nature.

Therefore, your new "morals" would be corrupted as follows:

- I am a family man, but

- I believe in taking care of the people I love

- I believe in being respectful and kind to everyone I meet

- I believe in helping people who are in need, giving back to society

- I don't like bullying, lying or dishonesty

- I love people who treat me kindly just as I treat them

Consider another example:

A person with low self-esteem should logically want to spend time around people who are up-building, kind and who butter up their ego.

However, that's not the "opposite" ego, is it? If you were truly exploring the opposite persona, you having low self-esteem would seek out someone who was not nice, but who demanded subservience and obedience. And in extreme cases, maybe you would even want that person to bully you. Because that reinforces your low confidence.

Not surprisingly, many subs find this a common desire when in a new relationship. They want someone to be aggressive, maybe even a little too aggressive. This is because…

Tip #21: You as a sub should want someone that communicates with your subconscious, not your conscious mind.

Your subconscious mind thinks the vulgar and offensive thoughts that your conscious mind tends to filter. Therefore, if your usual thought is "I am self-conscious about myself…" then logically you would want a person to say, "You should be confident, because you're beautiful and smart and wonderful!"

However, that's the conscious mind. Communicating with the unconscious mind would mean analyzing the person's thought process and telling them what they need to hear—even if it's illogical or destructive.

That's when the sub would hear something like:

"You are weak. You don't deserve my attention. You will do everything I say to please me and then I will decide if you're worthy."

Obviously, that's not healthy feel-good conversation you would ever hear in therapy! But there is something erotic about allowing yourself to feel natural—plagued with self-doubt perhaps—and then have all these nagging doubts confirmed.

Someone dominates you. Someone makes you feel unworthy...and then slowly makes you realize that the only way to escape these anxieties and self-doubts is to *fully submit* to the Dom's authority. That seems to bring you peace.

This might not make any logical sense but it's purposely illogical. It's emotional and it's working contrary to your morals and values. This is the "taboo" fantasy: doing the opposite of what you believe is moral.

Now granted, you will not be tempted to do everything that is destructive or exploitative. Some "sins" just may not tempt you whatsoever. In fact, it's safe to say that we only lust after what we feel we COULD actually accomplish, if only our morals weren't so high.

So no, most people won't have the desire to, say, streak naked and run through a football field on national television. It may be a "sin", (and yeah a few people have tried it!) but it's also likely not something you desire to do in real life, under any circumstances. It's not personally appealing to you, because it doesn't really speak to any hidden desires that you actually have.

Tip #22: Ask yourself if these taboo fantasies actually address a need or desire that you DO feel.

The more these fantasies actually address needs or wants, however suppressed, the hotter they will feel when you explore them. Your desires, apart from the "fantasy," may actually not be too far from normal.

For example:

- I want to feel attractive to other people

- I want more sexual experience

- I want more attention from an attractive mate

- I want more power in my relationship

- I want to feel more and think less

- I want to feel young again

- I want other people to think I'm dangerous

These are all fairly normal desires and not too shocking, right? So when you combine these DESIRES with your OPPOSITE persona, you have the recipe for a really hot taboo fantasy.

The new taboo fantasy consists of:

- I want to feel attractive to someone else. (DESIRE)

- My evil persona sometimes thinks about cheating on my spouse (OPPOSITE)

- The Taboo is now: an adulterous affair

Of course, cheating is actually one of the most common taboos in society and we have since discovered many other social dangers, and hot fantasies that are derived from dwelling on these dangerous thoughts.

Tip #23: Assign a value to each of these common "taboo" scenarios. Rate from 1 (not sexy at all) to 5 (really hot!).

- Sex With Strangers

- Race Play

- Master / Slave

- Cheating on a Spouse in secret, or in front of them

- Group Sex

- Bisexuality

- Religious Guilt

- Interracial Sex

- Violence in Foreplay

- Murder or Suicide Fantasy (i.e. choke play)

- Rape or Non-Consent (non-consent means coercion without physical violence, such as blackmail or mind control)

- Dirty Talking or Insults

- Voyeurism (watching other people naked or having sex)

- Exhibitionism (letting other people see you naked or having sex)

- Pregnancy (sex with a mother, breast feeding)

- Foot Fetish

- Bondage

- Scat Play or "Golden" Showers

- Sex during the woman's period

- Smoking

- Anal Play

Rather than stick to this basic list, create your own list of ideas and borrow from movies, erotica books, porn, and the stories of your friends (or Internet friends) on their most erotic experiences. Chances are, there are a number of fantasies you *haven't even thought of* that might be appealing to you, or your Dom.

One of the most important aspects of taboo sex is exposing yourself to new ideas and visualizing yourself engaging in unusual and uncharacteristic acts. That way you can decide if you feel attracted to the idea, moderate (meaning you may try it but might not like it) or are morally opposed to ever trying it.

You must learn these limits and probably as soon as possible, even before you trouble your Dom with this information. Though some Doms are eager to help, most of them will appreciate if you simply say upfront, "I do not like this...I do not want to experiment with that whatsoever."

Tip #24: Do leave room for exploration. Make sure you leave some taboos open for discussion.

Just because you've never thought about dirty talking or anal or being tied up, and you think they are intimidating, doesn't mean you would NEVER try them. It just means you need to approach them very cautiously and then wait and see how they feel after trying an exercise.

Many subs have found that with the right Dom, many taboo fantasies they never thought they would enjoy exploring, are actually very sexy in a scenario.

Now that you have the taboo fantasy, how do you actually explore it in BDSM? Do you or does your Dom take the lead in setting up the scene?

Chapter 5: Everyone Has Limits— What Are Yours?

It might seem reasonable that "harder and faster" is better when exploring sexual taboos, in reality the opposite is true. Though you can be very attracted to something, if that temptation is too extreme then your natural reaction will be to run away.

The same is true in BDSM and it's even worse if your Dom doesn't take your safety concerns seriously. Failure to care for a sub's physical and emotional health is a major mistake in the BDSM community and chances are that idiot Dom will quickly become blacklisted.

Going too hard or fast can be emotionally traumatizing to a person. Even if physical wounds heal quickly, emotional turmoil can very quickly become abuse in such a heated and intense situation.

While it IS the Dom's job to watch over you, you cannot assume that just any Dom is going to do the job right. At some point you must decide for yourself if the scene is going too far and if you are suffering in reality and experience real life pain, as opposed to kinky fun pain.

Once that boundary has been passed, it's time to end. And unfortunately for the Dom, he only gets one chance. Once he betrays your trust, there's no going back. So yes for the sake of the both of you...

Tip #25: Explain your limits and boundaries in advance, and write them down so you know for yourself what they are.

Everybody has limits and if you say that you don't, you are being dishonest. Everybody has limits because if they didn't they would literally be serial killers and sexual offenders not worthy of any trusts.

Don't discount your limits. The limits of both Dom and sub are what will eventually earn each other's trust. Ultimately, you will find that BDSM is not ALL about sex. Limits are simply human—our own moral compasses to life and they are very important to keep in mind.

Tip #26: You will never let your Dom decide your morals. Although you will obey him, you will only obey according to the conditions and limits you've both already agreed upon.

It's so much less trouble this way, when you agree and agree in writing. Otherwise, you really could be screwed up big time by a Dom who has no idea what he's doing.

So your limitations would look similar to your list of desires and taboos.

For example:

- Nothing to do with children

- Nothing to do with animals

- Nothing illegal

- No cutting

- No scat, vomit or urine

- No violence

- No crossing over into my "real life"

But you may go well beyond this list and create your own limits that every Dom has to abide by.

For example, you may not want to be "caged" overnight, or suffocated because of a health risk. Electrocution is very controversial among members, so all these are legitimate limits you might not want to surpass.

Soft Limits

Hard limits aside, you may also find that some limits will be reached DURING scene play. The truth is, even with a very good Dom, you may simply not be ready or able to endure some taboo fantasies or painful techniques—even if you find the idea appealing. And this is not the kind of thing you can "know" in advance, unless you actually experience displeasure and want to backtrack.

First understand that…

Tip #27: Finding a soft limit is not the Dom's fault or your fault. It is simply a discovery and it should be dealt with.

You may also find that not every "limit" you surpass has to be a painful or stressful experience. You may also find that you simply don't tolerate certain behaviors or types of Doms well. For instance, you may simply not like a Dom's voice, or a certain body type, or even the way a Dom touches you.

If you discover a turn off, then you either avoid the Dom altogether or avoid the action that makes you uncomfortable. You may also find that some Doms, even good ones, are just incompatible with you. Some Doms are not that interested in sexually pleasing some subs. Some Doms prefer only humiliation or pain and that's their limitation. That may or may not be compatible with your desires.

Usually soft limits are discovered when you "take a chance" and try a new activity or scenario that you are not sure about. You may be willing to try something new, perhaps something a little intimidating, and quickly find out that it either physically hurts or morally offends you.

And no, contrary to what some imposter Doms might think, you do NOT have to compromise in a BDSM relationship. You don't meet each other halfway, like a husband and wife do. This is not based on a marital romantic relationship. This is a relationship built on equal status, consensual role playing, and give and take with your partner.

Now while a couple can play BDSM games with each other, they cannot bring their BDSM into the marriage and "demand" that their partner compromise. BDSM exploration is not about compromising. It's about matching your partner and always respecting the other person's limits, hard or soft.

Communicating with Your Dom

Naturally, medical issues and triggers that cause real life pain or emotional distress must be mentioned in advance. Some Doms will ask for a checklist of activities (as previously discussed) for hard limits. Sometimes you will create a new checklist for soft limits. You may also find, usually through experimentation, that explaining why you don't like something is very effective; it makes an impact on the Dom, making sure he understands your motivations.

Now do keep in mind that:

Tip #28: Until your soft limits become hard limits, you must trust your Dom to push you just a little bit outside your usual comfort zone.

This element of "edging" and going a little bit farther each time is simply the sign of a good Dom. He knows how to push you according to what you can take, and he also knows when it's time to slow it down. True, you can send him signals if you feel the need. But until you send those signals, he will be pushing your limits. He will be studying your reaction.

The fact of the matter is, most subs love it when Doms push them. So as long as the Dom stays away from hard limits, soft limit pushing is encouraged, so as long as you don't find it stressful.

Expect the Dom to challenge your notions of comfort and your moral code. If there are soft limits you discover are too much, make this clear during the session, in the aftercare (out of character) and before the new session. You may even put it in writing.

Tip #29: Reevaluate your hard limit and soft limit list every so often.

Remember that you are a changing being in BDSM and what you don't like one day, may turn out to be very arousing the next day. Your desires change and are influenced by the Dom's curriculum. Therefore, don't be surprised if some of your hard limits change. You may even put a hard limit NO into a soft limit maybe category at some point. So as long as it's your decision and the Dom understands to take it slow, there's no reason you can't change your mind and redo your list.

An experienced Dom will know how to handle the situation and will not be intimidated if you change your mind and decide to try something new. A really good Dom may even play with your mind, threatening to surpass your hard limits just to get a reaction from you. He may not be planning to actually do that, but he's using the threat as a means of control. Some subs find this arousing, so as long as they trust the Dom and know he's not actually going to betray the trust. He is simply establishing power.

Punishment is another issue altogether. Whereas it's fairly easy to put the brakes on taboo fantasies, when pain enters the picture, it opens up a whole new Pandora's Box, if you will, and the repercussions can be extreme. Proceed to the next chapter with caution.

Chapter 6: Narrowing Down What Punishment You "Deserve"

It is slightly different comparing the exploration of fantasies with the exploration of pain. Pain must be explored with an almost doctor-like precision, so that the sub isn't gravely injured or emotionally raped.

Just because something is a fetish doesn't mean it should be explored. Maybe you've heard of sickening deep web stories about games that went too far or forums where cannibals and rapists meet together to discuss their predilections. This is not what BDSM is and without limits, and without a Dom you can trust, games can indeed spiral into madness.

This is why serious Doms and subs will adhere only to sessions that are safe, consensual and sane. When it comes to pain, there are many rules to follow in addition to the sub's own list of does and do nots.

Tip #30: Punishment doesn't accomplish much without training. Ask for the training and not the punishment.

Punishment for the sake of punishment doesn't do much of anything but inspire fear. It doesn't make the sub love the Dom any more. The punishment should be a natural result of disobedience OR conditioning, in an effort to change the thought process of the sub. Every last spanking or prick must be for a point. Doms are not causing pain randomly. Instead, they are conditioning you to change the way you think.

Now it is true that some subs just want punishment, perhaps because of guilt they feel or just a kink they enjoy. Even so, they are not being punished randomly. Instead, what the Dom usually does is organize sessions where they can expect to spanked, usually by planning and for a specific period of time.

The sub may enjoy the feeling of spontaneous punishment, but a really smart and mature Dom knows that these punishments work much better when they are organized and they help to influence how the sub thinks.

Therefore if you ask for training, then you will enjoy the rush of both pain and pleasure,

pleasure that comes when you do as you're told.

Limits can be set by the Dom or the sub, and you don't have to follow the Dom's orders if you think the punishment is becoming too rough or too random.

Different Types of Limits

There are actually a few types of limits to consider. For instance, as discussed in the previous chapter, soft limits are conditional. You may consent to certain activities but because you are hesitant about them there are strict conditions that must be followed. This may include prohibiting certain actions or taking scenes very slowly.

Hard limits should not be toyed with and sometimes these are not only personal but health-related. If you have a bad back or sensitive areas of your body, you may want to explicitly warn the Dom about going beyond these boundaries.

#31: Institute must-limits in addition to no! limits and soft limits.

Sometimes you forget that you as the sub have full power to demand must-limits, which are actions required if the Dom is going to exercise power over you. Once the Dom understands that these are "must" he will oblige. These requirement limits could be anything from the desire for aftercare, to "lots of breast play" or "lots of talking."

The fact that you make it a requirement must means these are crucial to the sessions being successful. If the Dom fails to do the requirement then he has betrayed you. There is no "forgetting" when you institute a "must-limit."

You should especially use requirement limits if you are allowing soft limits. For example, "I cannot have penetrative sex unless I spanked first." The Dom cannot just ignore the requirement limit and go for what he selfishly wants. The Dom does not have that power.

Time limits are also of great importance. Time limits during sessions of pain allow you to recover, or to enjoy the subspace chemicals. You cannot experience the high of subspace if you are constantly being punished. The "release" and holding of more punishment lets you feel the high, but only when you are given time to recover from the pain. Then pain continues when you are ready, usually in intervals of approximately 5-10 minutes of pain and then a few minutes of rest.

Tip #32: Make sure the scene has a time limit and the pain schedule has a time limit.

The Dom should handle this but if he doesn't volunteer the information, make sure he knows that this is your requirement. Scenes should last short time periods until you prove you are able to endure it for longer periods of time.

This may mean just 10-20 minutes to start with, and as you go along, make it longer, up to 60 minutes eventually. Remember, you can make as many sessions per week as you prefer, but taking your time in the beginning, with each session, is the safe way to start a new relationship.

Which also leads to:

Tip #33: Increase the length of foreplay to extend the scene and raise the level of anticipation.

This not only tests you to see if your heart and stomach can handle the pain, but you can also benefit from a greater endorphinal high. Much like foreplay enhances sex, stalling the scene and insisting that the Dom work his way up to the punishment with preparation and anticipation, will only help tickle your most taboo fantasies.

Tip #34: With your Dom determine how long this relationship should last.

Most in the community will insist on a re-lationship time limit for a full program or curriculum to run its course. This is not only prompt but also allows you to explore other BDSM relationships rather than just limiting yourself to one person.

The problem with untimed and indefinitely lasting relationships is that you can become romantically attached to your Dom the longer you stay, and considering that sex or pain is the only thing you have in common with each other, that relationship might not work out so well in "real life."

Besides, if you are new to BDSM and aren't that crazy about your Dom then don't limit yourself. Spread your wings and perhaps focus on other fantasies or experiences that you haven't tried yet. There's no sense in choosing the same Dom for every desire you have, since not all Doms will be experts at the same niche.

Tip #35: Make sure the Dom has a closure plan in place.

The Dom should plan for a mutually beneficial exit. In theory, all forms of therapy are temporary, even visiting a psychiatrist or psychologist. Spending too much time with a therapist (as in years on end) will eventually turn into an addiction—a surrogate drug that helps you cope, even though you learn nothing about how to cope on your own.

The same is true of the BDSM Dom-Sub relationship. It has to come to a natural end, especially considering the nature of BDSM which is: escalation. Each time you go to a session you are stimulated at a greater pace, eventually culminating in a subspace peak. There's really nowhere to go beyond that, besides back down into the natural world. You cannot keep escalating or else the relationship will have to progress to severe levels.

But what if you really do love the time you spend with your Dom and you can't seem to break away?

This type of relationship can be dangerous and definitely unusual…but it's not out of the question. Let's discuss this in more detail in Chapter 7.

Chapter 7: The Scale of BDSM, From Bottom to Slave

We know that *bottom* and *sub* means the subservient partner. And you may understand that a *slave* is an even more devoted sub, well beyond the usual definitions. But you still may not understand how a slave and Master dynamic works.

For starters, realize that most slaves start off as bottoms or subs, and simply meet a Dom that can take care of their immediate needs. However, this grows into something more intense than just a desire that needs satiated.

Let's say that you've fallen hard for your Dom and don't want to lose him. What's next?

Tip #36: Determine whether the Dom feels the same way.

If not, then you may just be in need of another Dom, and more pleasure or pain, but not necessarily with *him*. Subs can trade off Doms, even if they enjoy the same activity. Doms are respectful of one another and will give referrals to people they trust.

If by some chance your Dom feels the same intensity and love (even though it may not be romantic love, mind you) then you could continue the relationship indefinitely as a slave. If a sub and Dom feel intensely about each other, they can progress to the more extreme level of 24-7 ownership, or a master-slave relationship.

The difference is that the dominant-submissive model is based on love and training. The Dom trains you to help recondition your mind, or give you pleasure and pain for a specific goal. The slave, on the other hand, loves the Master so much that service and obedience is its own reward. The Master owns the slave as property, even though the sub still may "control" the relationship.

The point is she is so willing to do the Master's bidding that the relationship has evolved to the point beyond traditional BDSM power exchanges.

Tip #37: Consensual slavery bends the rules, so find a Dom you can trust exclusively and who never disappoints. If you want to try this relationship, put a time limit on it just to make sure you are happy.

The Dom you fancy should be very trustworthy, to the point where this is (almost) a romantic relationship, at least to the extent that it involves your monogamy. These master-slave relationship do not necessarily involve sexual or pleasure-pain acts, like a traditional session would.

There are no limits, no time frames—just the control that the Master wields over you. You crave his control so much you consensually agree to be his for all hours of the day and indefinitely until one of you decides to end the relationship.

Sometimes slaves are masochists and enjoy the Master mistreating them. For example:

- Ordering them to do chores and providing free service

- Humiliating tactics, especially among others, which gives the slave a high

- Sexual or pleasure-pain tactics, whenever the master chooses

- Making them stay monogamous even though the Master sees other subs

- Lending the slave out to other Doms or other lovers

Obviously, this type of relationship isn't for everybody and it's actually discouraged for newcomers to BDSM, since trust is not so easily earned in this lifestyle. It usually takes years for a sub to trust a Dom this greatly.

The more extreme and long-term the relationship is, the less it is "role playing" and the more it resembles, simply, a submissive lifestyle. It resembles a traditional marriage in that the couple are committed to each other and there are fewer "rules" to follow; mostly just mutual trust. Of course, it's far from a traditional modern marriage since the Master wields almost complete power over the slave.

And although the slave still has the choice to leave the Master at any time, this lifestyle really is not based on the traditional equal power share between Doms and subs. In BDSM, the subs make decisions and the Doms seek to please them. But in consensual slavery, the Master decides what to do with the slave and the slave usually tolerates the behavior because of love.

Tip #38: IF you decide to take a Master, show your declaration of love.

Slaves don't have rings, but they can show their allegiance to their master by wearing a collar, or being listed in a slave register or perhaps even changing their name to appease the Master. Some Masters arrange for ceremonies. Some may even brand or tattoo their name on the slave's body.

Tip #39: This is not all fun and games. The Master will try to change you. And you will try to change yourself to please him.

There are any number of ceremonies that may follow a commitment and much like a marriage this relationship is witnessed by friends. The collar can be neckwear or a bracelet or jewelry piece, and symbolizes the slave title.

The slave training process, even if it develops from a long BSDM Dom-sub relationship, is a learning process. The training is outlined in steps and this is then finalized with a slave contract.

Tip #40: If you're going to play extreme, be explicit in the contract.

In a slave relationship, have the Dom detail expectations as far as chores and domestic requirements such as grooming.

Many master-slave relationships also have contractual terms on deference, language, sex, choice of clothing and how the dynamic operates outside the home around others. All of these rules are actually for training, since the master is teaching the slave a new identity, one that involves thinking, speaking and behaving in a way pleasing to the Master—not the slave's natural personality.

In response to good slave behavior, the Master provides lodging. Therefore, you may occasionally see some ads for master-slave unions on Craigslist and the like. They will often speak of living arrangements and the basic needs they provide as a reward for good behavior in living with the Master and or his other slaves.

Another phase of master-slave relationships is the "total power" or "consensual nonconsent" session, which is where the Master has complete power and plays with "no set limits" and no safe words.

This tends to lead to extremes and so tends to be frowned upon by most members of BDSM community. This dynamic would only happen in a non-traditional master-slave relationship, and is also called *edgeplay*. This flies in the face of Safe, Sane and Consensual play, as well as the Risk Aware Consensual Kink mission of the BDSM lifestyle.

Tip #41: Avoid edgeplay and Doms who seem to think they're entitled to edgeplay with you because you're just not ready.

In fact many edgeplay activities are controversial, whether it's erotic asphyxiation, fire play, gun play or knife play. Not only is bloodletting dangerous, but there is also an increased risk of STD transmission with multiple partners, not to mention seroconverting disease when bodily fluid is recklessly exchanged.

No limit edgeplay should only be attempted by experienced Doms and a Dom / Master you trust after a long relationship. Remember, you can always frame the scene to look like non-consent as a kink, even though you can detail in the contract your limits and time schedule.

Which brings up an interesting point: *how can you tell if you've been with a good Dom, an OK Dom or a complete psycho posing as a Dom?*

In the next chapter, we'll discuss the warning signs you as a smart sub should know.

Chapter 8: Common Mistakes Subs Make

Beginner subs usually make the same mistakes every time:

- They trust the wrong Dom

- They let the Dom push them too far

- They don't have written contracts

- They don't detail or make the Dom detail the program, including the time and limits

- They don't have "soft limits" and thus can't expand beyond the threshold because of inhibition

- They tell the Dom what to do rather than let the Dom guide them

Let's first focus on what could be a huge and potentially life threatening mistake: choosing a poor quality Dom.

Tip #42: Try to categorize each type of Dom you meet so that you will immediately know who is a threat by red flag behaviors.

Consider the archetypical Doms you meet. While abusive female Doms tend to be fewer than males, it's not unheard of to find a psychotic female Dom so the same warnings are fit for male subs.

Types of Doms to Beware of

Creepy Guy Dom

How to spot him a mile away:

- Brags

- Is more of an asshole than someone who makes you feel protected

- He demands you call him by a title as soon as you meet

- He describes how to please him without the two of you discussing a contract

- He ignores limits and safe words

- He lies, especially about his friends in the BDSM community—if he has any

- Which reminds us of another red flag…he has no friends

- He is more concerned with his own pleasure than your needs

- He makes you feel bad about yourself. No real Doms do this UNLESS instructed by the sub first

- He isolates you from friends and family

- He tries to imply you're not a good submissive

Although subs do make mistakes, face it. Any Dom who tries to talk down to you and tell you that you're not doing it "right"— you're not exploring your own fantasies in the "right" way, is full of crap. This is supposed to be all about you.

The Predator Dom

This guy is actually not as bad as the Creepy Dom because he does somewhat understand the BDSM community and standards. However, he is usually overcompensating for his own lack of experience or lack of training. For this reason he is very attracted to new subs, since experienced subs know better than to waste time with him.

The problem is he lies often just to flatter his own ego. It's much better to be HONEST and to find a sub/Dom that is at your own level or that is wiser than you, to help guide you to a higher level. Preying upon the newcomers is not an entirely honest thing to do.

The Collector Dom

This Dom has experience, even though he's not exactly a master performer. He simply loves working with new subs because they are innocent and easily impressed. He is the classic Christian Grey archetype—trying to get back the innocent that he lost.

Some subs also describe these Doms as chronically "distracted" by other subs they keep or happen to meet. They are not dangerous but are often the WRONG type of relationship for a beginning sub. She falls in love with him even though he is emotionally unavailable.

The Experienced Dom

This is who you want to meet—he's stable, mature, friendly and a master performer once the contract is signed.

The problem is not necessarily him but YOU.

Tip #43: Do not fall in love with your Dom.

This bears repeating because so many subs make this mistake. Even if you don't plan on feeling anything or falling in love, you must comprehend the strong emotional attachment that usually happens after your initial sessions. The experiences are oftentimes mind-blowing and more intense than you've ever felt.

You may think that because it was so good for you, it was also good for the Dom. And yes, he may have enjoyed it but don't assume that he felt it as intensely as you did. Strong shared experiences doesn't mean that you are soul mates and sad to say, subs usually don't turn their Doms into husbands.

The dynamic just isn't right and it's very difficult to combine both "worlds."

Remember that he's already done this with many other subs and so you aren't special.

This is why it's doubly important to make sure the Dom has a TIME LIMIT on the relationship and that he is organized, with a plan on training you until the natural end of the session.

Doms that are naturally gifted but who do not have a plan, will often do more damage to their sub because they don't care for them and don't leave them on a positive note. Not only is immediate aftercare important, session by session, but long-term aftercare, as in helping the sub to reconcile the relationship, is essential to helping your sub better herself.

Tip #44: Participate in the Community...or at least a friend.

One of the most neglected needs for subs (and especially new subs) is that they isolate themselves from others, whether their friends or the BDSM community. They want their privacy and that's understandable. But what happens when something goes wrong, and no one outside of that room knows anything about it?

This doesn't necessarily mean encountering insane wannabe Doms, but it could also include the Dom falling unconscious, or a fire starting, or someone having a medical emergency. What if one of you is tied up and the Dom goes missing? Who is going to untie you?

All of this could be prevented if only more subs started talking frankly with their friends about the activity, or if that's not feasible, then make some new friends with other nearby subs to keep check on each other. This is common sense and can go a long way in watching out for your fellow man.

In the next chapter, we're going to discuss an important issue regarding safety and communication but from the angle of "in session."

Chapter 9: You're in Control— How to "Train" Your Master

This may seem like a confusing thought, since your Dom is supposed to be the one training you. And yes, that's usually how it happens when you meet the right Dom who combines maturity and experience with his own unique brand of zeal.

But here's a question. What if you meet a Dom that you like, and although he's not perfect, he does seem to give you what you need in terms of pain and pleasure? Maybe he just needs some encouragement.

Well, encouragement is the sub's way of training the Dom. By your performance, you can help this newcomer reach his peak and become the best at what he does. In the end, it will help BOTH of you.

Tip #45: Help him understand your needs and his needs.

The most common error in BDSM is when the Dom doesn't understand what the sub needs. He may not even understand himself or why he's doing this. This will instantly create a problem in session.

The Confused Dom, who is earnest, will probably spend too much time acting a role that he thinks you want, but that is way off the charts. This role is usually the alpha male, the asshole and the selfish prick. These characteristics do occasionally come up in play, but they are not the true "motivation." The Dom's motivation is something directly related to the process of learning, of sharing and negotiation, and of contractual explanations.

Sometimes a verbal discussion is the best way to explain your needs, expectations and the Dom's requirements. You can talk out your concerns, give specifics and see if the Dom actually understands why these scenes are necessary and why they are pleasurable.

Tip #46: Give him specific reasons why your limits are what they are and why you're attracted to certain scenes and behaviors.

This helps immensely because Doms, and especially men, respond better to visuals and specific examples, along with a logical progression of thoughts. They need strong reminders and they need to be told WHY something is the way it is.

For instance, this is a common fetish that subs may have: a *teacher-student fantasy*.

The man's natural inclination might be to be an aggressive-minded, dirty-talking teacher because that's what he thinks the sub wants. However, if he actually takes the time to talk to the sub, write a contract and verbally discuss the scenarios in negotiation he would discover the truth.

The sub says: *"I want to be seduced, not smacked around. The teacher must not be too aggressive or foul-mouthed. Because what turns me on is the realism. If this were happening in reality, a teacher would not risk getting caught being a sex-crazed animal. Instead, he would discipline me with a soft but strong voice and tell me what I'm doing wrong. He would speak innocently of what I'm feeling and what he's feeling, so that I'm not sure what we're doing is wrong."*

The sub would go on to list requirement limits:

- No dirty talking or use of the word "slut"

- No references to sucking him off

- He doesn't use the word "ass" or "pussy" – he uses euphemisms

- When he spanks me he says it's for my own good, very loving

And so on. As you can see, the sub went out of her way to explain what she wants and why she wants it just so. She didn't just expect the Dom to get it right the first time.

Tip #47: Overplay your part...make yourself feel it.

The bottom line is that the Dom responds to what you give him in performance. You cannot take a passive attitude and just "obey" the Dom without giving him the intense feelings that he wants to see.

Now this doesn't mean you should fake orgasm or pretend to like something even if you don't like it. This simply means that you react and play up your emotions just a little bit. Show off and moan at a higher volume than average. The more excited you "play" the more your emotions will be involved, and eventually you will feel heightened sexual or pain-pleasure response.

In simpler words, don't just lie back and experience. Help your Dom by giving him the same ENERGY that he is giving you. When he disciplines you SHOW IT. MEAN IT. And respond with power, with voice and with movement. After a while, you won't be faking anything and will feel a new peak of excitement.

Tip #48: Tell your Dom when it feels really good...but be less enthused when he does something you don't like.

While this is a bit manipulative, it may be necessary if you're working with new Doms who haven't quite had the experience to please you the way you like. (And sometimes an OK Dom is better than no Dom) So here's how you "train them" to give a better performance.

You start by giving them more energy, voice and dialog ("yes master, or "yes please spank me!" and so on) only when he is disciplining you the way you like. When he does something right, let him know by being loud and obvious. You don't have to fake orgasmic noises but you should be vocal and be expressive. This will "reward" him for his efforts and he will know what to keep doing to make you experience even more intense feelings.

On the other hand, "punish him" when he does something you don't like. You can punish him by muting your voice, giving him less of a reaction or not responding at all. This is a great way to send him negative signals to try something else—but without breaking the mood or reducing tension by breaking character.

It's true—breaking character by using clinical terms or criticizing the Dom's technique is very unsexy and perhaps insulting to him. You should only do this if he has betrayed your trust and broken one of your NO Limits. And if that's the case, it's probably just time to end it because he obviously disregarded your rules.

However, if he is merely trying something that you don't like, but that wasn't previously agreed upon, then the best thing to do is just stay in character and stop responding. He will get the hint. Or, you can use the safe word which instructs him to stop or go slower.

If you really want to show encouragement, tell him how good his work was in the after-care and discussion phase, following the scene and even before the scene begins. This will boost his ego a little bit, and so long as he's still pleasing you a little ego stroking will only help.

Your role as the sub is always one of sub-mission, so in reality when you "train" your Dom or Master, you are only helping him learn to be a better Dom. You are NOT usurping his position as teacher because there is no Dom vs. Dom in BDSM, not in the classic definition.

This leads us to the next important tip…

Tip #49: Do NOT manipulate the Dom and tell him what to do.

This is counterproductive because then you're just "topping from the bottom," an expression that means you're disrespecting the Dom's role and are just basically treating the Dom like a sub, telling him what you want but *not letting him plan according to his own creativity and intelligence*.

If you keep telling the Dom what to do, essentially thinking for him and taking away his freedom to experiment within the guidelines, you are manipulating him. These type of imposter subs do sometimes pop up and they are very difficult to get along with.

In fact, their entire motivation might simply be to destroy other Doms because they simply love their real Master so much...OR they are just incapable of being a sub and should probably stick to being a Dom.

Tip #50: Do not try to get a specific reaction from the Dom and this includes begging for punishment.

You really shouldn't challenge the Dom. Sometimes trouble making subs will break their own rules or surpass the Dom's rules so they can be punished. This is not going to work because you're already betraying the Dom's trust. He has every right to leave you for this manipulative attitude.

Instead of being a bitchy sub here's an idea...

Tip #51: Simply tell the Dom that you want attention and punishment rather than throwing a fit.

Immature subs throw tantrums and break rules. But respectful subs merely ASK for what they want. If they want punishment they ask for it. And they can even tell the Dom to explain why the punishment is coming—because the sub feels neglected or feels rebellious. When you just tell the Dom you want to act out and be punished the Dom can work with that.

When you play mind games with the Dom, it's just confusing and perhaps even hurtful to him, since he's trying his best to give you what you SAY you want—not what you're thinking.

Having said all that, the truth is you will never truly know the joy of good BDSM pain and pleasure until you find the right Dom that can train YOU—not you have to guide him.

So our next chapter will be all about where to find your first Great Dom!

Chapter 10: How Picky Should You Be in Looking for a Dom?

The right type of Dom is worth waiting for. We can guarantee you one thing—as soon as you decide you want to be involved in BDSM play, you will get lots of offers. Women are very popular in BDSM and submissive gay men are too among Doms. Straight men, well…let's just say you really got to work hard or pay big bucks to find a woman who really connects with you. Because the truth is there are just way too many bad quality wannabe male Doms out there.

The point is that you have to get it through your head that the first few Doms that come along are probably going to be bad news. BDSM is rising in popularity and a lot of men out there think they can increase their chances of getting laid if they just pretend to be a Dom.

Tip #52: Start by creating a system of filtering out the wrong types of Doms. Learn to say no and stick to it.

We already told you which kind were bad news so officially create your protocol and decide in advance what you'll say or how many "strikes" they get. Usually a one strike policy will do because real Doms just don't say stupid things.

You have to get used to saying NO now, as you negotiate, because you will meet plenty of pushy people and later, in a session, is NOT the time to second-guess the relationship.

Tip #53: Get connected to your local BDSM community or use a website like Fetlife or another special interesting matching site to look around.

Search for someone closest to your location. Rather than chatting with random strangers, spend some time posting messages and getting to know various people in message threads, local announcements, movie and book reviews, and the like. This endears you to the community and will certainly help in attracting more quality Doms.

Patience is a virtue and you should understand that it does take some time. When you actually become part of the community, and not part of the Craigslist imposter Dom rejects, you will quickly find that there are probably more serious subs than there are quality Doms.

In order to attract the attention of a popular and very well reviewed Dom, you have to…

Tip #54: Stand out from among the crowd of inferior subs.

This means not only are you looking for quality, but you must do your best to showcase what a good sub you are and how deserving you are of attention. Some of the most common mistakes new subs make include:

- Being whiny or juvenile in trying to attract Dom attention

- Pestering Doms in private messages or forums

- Being impatient

- Manipulating the Dom

- Treating Doms like subs—not showing proper respect!

Sometimes it takes months or years to find a Dom you really click with. For the best results, be choosy. The sooner you settle, the worst experience you're going to have.

Another reason you should try to talk to the community is that Doms themselves talk a lot to other Doms—not just subs. In fact, Doms that isolate themselves from the community are usually not seen as trustworthy. Doms, like subs, put out a watch for troublemaking subs and word spreads quickly.

Tip #55: Show respect immediately once you engage a Dom in conversation.

This means you call them by their preferred title and take an interest in their conversation, hobbies and profile. Showing respect doesn't mean flirting or engaging in sexual dialog—this comes later. A Dom will give you a questionnaire to see if you're a good match.

Tip #56: Check to see if you are actually COMPATIBLE with your Dom according to their profile and questionnaire.

Many new subs are oblivious to publicly posted information and this tends to annoy Doms. Treat the experience like a job application and take it seriously, rather than thinking of the whole thing as a hook up or as a cyber fling.

Do You Have Standards When You're a Sub?

You should because having good taste in Doms, means you will more than likely have a better first session. Talking with the natives of your local BDSM community will help you to learn the lifestyle and avoid troublesome Doms and predators.

In fact, it's often suggested that you talk with the community – such as at local MUNCH functions (which are meet and greets where people show up in normal clothing and just casually chat) rather than single out one Dom and focus all your attention on them.

Tip #57: Don't give out much in the way of personal information at first, but do strike up conversation and learn about your new friends.

This is the time to learn so be opened to learn from everybody, while not revealing too much about yourself. The more you reveal, the less mystery you project; and the more you can be taken advantage of, as well.

A lot of good Doms will be respectful in the beginning and may even be too nice or unassuming because they want to be friends first, and Dom-sub friends later. More aggressive Doms, especially the ones who try to take up all your time and attention, are typically bad news.

Tip #58: Beware of Doms who can't laugh or who brag too much about strange things.

This is easy to remember outside of the BDSM community but once you're inside you may come to expect the unexpected and forgive some things that members are doing. Not smart, considering that humorless or overly aggressive Doms, or Doms that make up stories about being part of a special club or elite membership, are usually trouble.

What's more important to get to know is how many meetings he attends, what his interests are outside of the lifestyle, and just how experienced a Dom he is.

Believe it or not, some of the top Doms actually do give speeches, write books and serve as "officers" at group events. They take this seriously because they have the experience that you want.

Doms that are overly negative about other members also tend to be problematic. Some subs have discovered that simply watching the Dom in a non-kink setting—such as a restaurant where he deals with other people—is a good sense of what the Dom is like behind closed doors.

If he treats others with respect, he will likely be a loving and respectful Dom.

Tip #59: Don't believe everything you hear.

Curiously, the BDSM community occasionally has bitter feuds happening between highly opinionated people. Therefore, it is not uncommon to find that two Doms – each of which are trusted by the majority – are not fond of each other. There may even be warnings sent out to newcomers after a feud happens that forces various members to take sides.

Just remember that there are two sides to every story and rather than accept anything and everything that is said about someone, the best thing to do is compare both sides of the story to get some kind of congruity and understanding of what happened between them. You can also ask others who they believe and why.

Many members may be quick to defend someone they have had good dealings with, even if others in the community are issuing warnings. That's just human nature and there are bound to be clashes in any community involving "big" alpha personalities.

Tip #60: Befriend other submissives first.

Frankly this is the VIP pass you need to have a good first experience. Submissives, oftentimes women, will befriend fellow subs and will also "take them under their wing" so to speak. They want your first experience to be good and will take an interest in steering you clear of any trouble.

They can also provide advice on how to get along with certain Doms and what these Doms prefer to see from new subs. They may even be able to put in a good word for you with one of their Doms.

Always ask questions as to why they like a Dom, or don't like him, or ideas for scenes that have worked brilliantly in their own experience.

Tip #61: Play the field and don't commit to just one person.

If you really want to sample the best while still staying to yourself, attend a Group Play Party, which allows you to casually play with Doms or subs (or watch if you're shy) so that you can see how they work in real time without the heavy pressure of a one on one scene.

Proper Etiquette for Firing Your Dom

At some point you may discover that the Dom's relationship isn't working out. However, this Dom hasn't intentionally broken any limits or rules, nor has he been a poor quality Dom. He simply didn't "click" with you and it's no one's fault. How do you break up the relationship early and ahead of schedule?

Granted, you do owe your long-term Dom some explanation, rather than a Creepy Dom whom you just met and who is being rude.

Tip #62: Start by focusing on what you did appreciate and what you learned from him.

It's simply courteous to focus on the positives before delivering bad news later on. Butter him up a little at first and then list the positives of what you experienced.

Tip #63: Say that you simply did not achieve what you hoped to achieve and that it was no one's fault. Just an incompatible match.

The more specifics you provide the better because vaguely worded rejections usually only provoke the other party who wants to "fix it." State what you were expecting, what occurred and why you didn't like it.

If the reason the relationship went south was because of repeated mistakes the Dom was making, tell him that and be perfectly honest. You are not in character and do not have to lie or submit to his authority. You are simply communicating honestly and letting him know for his own self-improvement what he could work on in his future relationships.

Tip #64: If he seems standoffish start telling him that you have been doing research into BDSM and have talked to others before making this decision.

Showing him that this is not an emotional decision, nor is it a case of punishing him for a single wrongdoing. It is simply a truth you have observed over quite some time and not just one session.

Tip #65: Be blunt, be concise and do not draw the argument out.

The more you argue the more the unhappy Dom will try to convince you to try again. Instead, state in certain terms that you have made your decision and that you don't want him contacting you again. Do not give false assurances that things could continue "IF"…because this will string him along and send mixed signals.

Be Helpful!

When you've gained experience and made new friends, BE A FRIEND! Volunteer your time, opinion and energy to helping your fellow subs and Doms with their relationship problems. There is nothing secretive about this community. Everyone is eager to make new friends and have discussions about their experiences. You may even find that the more you learn, the more you can help teach new subs how to properly enjoy their first time!

Conclusion

We've come to the end of this book and have discussed ways to fully enjoy taboo fantasies, bear down and take the pain, and find the Dom that really rocks your world.

The last piece of advice we can offer you as your sub training begins is...

Tip #66: Get your emotions involved. Don't be afraid to let go and be RAW.

BDSM scenarios are a form of method acting. You are not merely pretending to play a character for the camera, and not even for the Dom's sake.

You are putting yourself into the character and calling upon your own buried emotions, suppressed desires, and uncharacteristic thoughts. The more of "you" you put into this performance, rather than doing what you think the Dom wants to see, the more you will enjoy it.

This doesn't mean faking anything or being passive. This means that you act like yourself, you naturally approach the scene—but according to how the Dom guides you. He will bring thoughts and feelings out of you that you never even knew you had, as long as you can allow yourself to be guided. Trust is everything here and surrendering your mind and body to a trusted friend is the best way to discover something new about yourself.

Don't be afraid of misbehaving or embarrassing yourself or being too raw or emotive. That is good.

Some people cry, some people scream and some people experience orgasmic joy greater than regular sex could ever provide. And they were allowed to feel it because they left their inhibitions behind.

So don't hold on, and DON'T overly guard yourself. Once you find someone you can trust, give him everything and let him direct you into a great and natural performance for the ages.

However, our BDSM Sub Training course is far from over.

In the next book, we are going to discuss some specifics on how Doms use TOYS and other supplies, and how this dynamic makes our scenarios so titillating. Learn what to expect and how to prepare yourself for extreme emotional peaks in the next book.

Other Books by Matthew Larocco

 Dom's Guide To BDSM Vol. 1: 49 Must-Know Tips On How To Be The Perfect Dom/Master Your Submissive Will Truly Respect & Admire

 Dom's Guide To BDSM Vol. 2: 71 Submissive Training & Reconditioning Tips Any Dom/Master Must Know

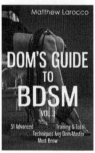 Dom's Guide To BDSM Vol. 3: 51 Advanced Submissive Training & Total Dominance Techniques Any Dom/Master Must Know